Everyman's Poetry

Everyman, I will go with thee, and be thy guide

Apollinaire

Edited and translated by ROBERT CHANDLER

EVERYMAN
J. M. Dent · London

This edition first published by Everyman Paperbacks in 2000

J. M. Dent
Orion Publishing Group
Orion House
5 Upper St Martin's Lane
London WC2H 9EA

Typeset by Deltatype Ltd, Birkenhead, Merseyside
Printed in Great Britain by
The Guernsey Press Co. Ltd, Guernsey, C. I.

British Library Cataloguing-in-Publication
Data is available on request

ISBN 0 460 88211 2

Contents

Part Three: Poems Written 1914–18

Note on the Author and Translator

GUILLAUME APOLLINAIRE was born in Rome in 1880, the son of Angelica de Kostrowitzky, an aristocratic Polish adventuress, and – probably – an Italian army officer. In 1887, however, Angelica, Guillaume and Guillaume's half-brother, Alberto, all moved to Monaco. Guillaume was educated there and in Nice. In 1901, after supporting himself in Paris as a literary hack, Guillaume took on a job in the Rhineland as tutor to the daughter of a German widow. There he fell in love with the English governess, Annie Playden. During the same year he adopted the name of Apollinaire. In 1905, back in Paris, he first met Picasso and Max Jacob. He was to remain close to nearly all the important painters of the day, writing enthusiastically about Cubism and other avant-garde movements. In 1911 Apollinaire was briefly imprisoned, wrongly suspected of having stolen the *Mona Lisa*. His most famous book, *Alcohols*, was published in 1913. In December 1914 Apollinaire enlisted. Officially he was still of Russian nationality, so this was a demonstration of allegiance to his adopted country. He served first in the artillery, then in the infantry. In March 1916 he was wounded in the head; the initial operation was followed by a trepannation. During the rest of the war he worked in Paris. *Calligrams*, the innovative volume containing most of his war poetry, was published in April 1918. Apollinaire married Jacqueline Kolb in May 1918, but died during the 'flu epidemic in November.

ROBERT CHANDLER's translations of Sappho are also published in the Everyman's Poetry series. His translations of French, Italian and Russian poetry have appeared in the journal *Modern Poetry in Translation*, and his own poems have been published in the *Spectator* and the *London Magazine*. He has also translated, and co-translated, the work of the Russian prose-writers Vasily Grossman and Andrey Platonov.

Chronology of Apollinaire's Life

Year	*Age*	*Life*
1880		Guglielmo de Kostrowitzky born on 26 August at 5 a.m. in Rome. His mother was Angelica de Kostrowitzky; his father was probably an Italian army officer, Francesco Flugi d'Aspermont
1882	2	Birth of Apollinaire's brother, or half-brother, Alberto
1887	7	The de Kostrowitzky family move to Monaco, where Angelica, now calling herself Olga, seems to have supported herself as a casino hostess and courtesan. Apollinaire attends the Collège Saint-Charles
1896	16	The Collège Saint-Charles is closed down. Apollinaire commutes to the Collège Stanislas in Cannes, also run by the Marianist fathers
1897	17	Apollinaire commutes to the French secular lycée in Nice
1899	19	A Belgian newspaper reports that Apollinaire and his brother have, without paying the bill, left the hotel where they had spent the previous three months. They had been installed there by Jules Weil, their

Chronology of his Times

Year	*Cultural Context*	*Historical Events*
1880	Deaths of Flaubert and George Eliot	First Boer War
1886	Birth of Siegfried Sassoon	
1887	Birth of Rupert Brooke and Saint-John Perse. Death of Jules Laforgue	Queen Victoria's Golden Jubilee
1889	Swinburne, *Poems and Ballads*	Birth of Adolf Hitler
1890		First underground railway in London
1891	Death of Arthur Rimbaud	
1892	Death of Tennyson	
1893	Birth of Wilfred Owen	
1895	Wilde, *The Importance of Being Earnest*	Marconi's 'wireless' telegraphy
1896	Housman, *A Shropshire Lad.* Death of Verlaine	
1897	Louis Aragon and Paul Éluard born	
1899	Freud, *The Interpretation of Dreams*. Death of Mallarmé	Second Boer War

		mother's lover. A month later, before a magistrate in Paris, Apollinaire professes amazement: 'I fail to understand why we should be accused of fraud'
1901	21	Apollinaire publishes his first poems, over the name Kostrowitzky, in *La Grande France*. He has been living in Paris, supporting himself through badly paid office work and writing pulp fiction. In August he takes on a job in the Rhineland as tutor to the daughter of the Vicomtesse de Milhau, the German widow of a Frenchman. He falls in love with an English governess, Annie Playden, and is fiercely jealous, threatening to kill her when she refuses his offer of marriage. After a visit to the Apollinariskirche at Remagen he adopts the name 'Apollinaire'; his original baptism certificate referred to his mother as 'daughter of Apollinaris, of St Petersburg'
1903	23	Visits London to see Annie Playden
1904	24	Second visit to London. Alarmed by the violence of his jealous threats, Annie finds herself a job as a governess in the States. On his return to Paris, Apollinaire completes two major poems, both inspired by Annie: 'La Chanson du Mal-Aimé' and 'L'Émigrant de Landor Road'. First meeting with Vlaminck and Dérain
1905	25	First meeting with Picasso and Max Jacob. Publishes admiring articles about Picasso
1907	27	Meets Braque and brings him to Picasso's studio

1901		Death of Queen Victoria; accession of Edward VII
1902		Second Boer War ends
1903		Wright brothers make first powered flight; suffragette movement in UK
1904	Chekhov, *The Cherry Orchard*	
1906	Galsworthy, *The Man of Property*	
1907	Picasso, *Les Demoiselles d'Avignon*	
1909	Ezra Pound, *Personae*	Ford's Model T car; Blériot flies across English Channel

1911	31	Publishes first volume of poetry, *Le Bestiaire*, with woodcuts by Raoul Dufy. In September Apollinaire is wrongfully arrested, suspected of having stolen the *Mona Lisa* from the Louvre. The reason for his being suspected was the discovery that a casual friend of his had previously stolen some Iberian statuettes and sold them to Picasso. The affair leaves Apollinaire profoundly disturbed, all the more so because Picasso appears, under interrogation, to have been equivocal in his support. Soon after Apollinaire's release, his relationship with the painter Marie Laurencin comes to an end. They had been involved since 1907
1913	33	Publishes not only 'MÉDITATIONS ESTHÉTIQUES: *Les Peintres Cubistes*', but also his most famous volume of poetry: *Alcohols*
1914	34	Apollinaire volunteers on 10 August; officially he is still considered of Russian nationality because of his mother, and therefore not obliged to enlist. His second application, in December, is accepted, and he joins the artillery. Begins his affair with Lou, to whom he sends seventy-six love poems between October 1914 and September 1915
1915	35	Meets Madeleine on 1 January; becomes engaged to her in December. During the year he sends many of the same love poems to both her and Lou

1910	Deaths of Mark Twain and Tolstoy; Yeats, *Responsibilities and Other Poems*	Death of Edward VII and accession of George V; Post-Impressionist exhibition in London
1911		Amundsen reaches South Pole
1912	*Georgian Poetry 1911–12*; Jung, *The Psychology of the Unconscious*	Balkan Wars; loss of the *Titanic*
1913	D. H. Lawrence, *Sons and Lovers* Stravinsky, *Rite of Spring*	Woodrow Wilson US President; opening of Panama Canal
1914	Joyce, *Dubliners* Yeats, *Responsibilities* Frost, *North of Boston*	Outbreak of First World War; battle of Mons
1915	Death of Rupert Brooke	Gallipoli campaign; loss of the *Lusitania*

1916	36	Wounded above the right temple by shell splinters on 17 March. The splinters were removed the next morning. A further operation, a trepannation, is carried out in early May. Apollinaire breaks with Madeleine. For the remainder of the war, he works in the Censor's Office and the Ministry of Colonies
1917	37	First performance of Apollinaire's *drama surréaliste, Les Mamelles de Tirésias.* Apollinaire had recently invented the term '*sur-réalisme*'.
1918	38	Publishes *Calligrams* on 15 April. Marries Jacqueline Kolb on 2 May. Still not released from the army, he is promoted in July to first lieutenant
		Dies of 'flu on 9 November

1916	Joyce, *A Portrait of the Artist as a Young Man*	Battles of Verdun and the Somme; Easter Rising in Dublin
1917	T. S. Eliot, *Prufrock and Other Observations* Kafka, *Metamorphosis* Death of Edward Thomas, 7 May	October Revolution in Russia; battles of Arras and Passchendaele; United States enters First World War
1918	Deaths of Isaac Rosenberg and Wilfred Owen Rupert Brooke, *Collected Poems* Sassoon, *Counter Attack* Hopkins, *Poems*	First World War ends on 11 November
1919		Treaty of Versailles

Introduction

Apollinaire stands at the end of one tradition and at the beginning of another. He is a romantic, a lover of grace and beauty who was unable to stomach the naturalism of Maupassant or Zola. He has been described as 'the last of the poets whose lines young people know by heart, one of the most French of our poets, in the pure tradition of Villon, of La Fontaine, of Gérard de Nerval, of Baudelaire, of Verlaine'.[1] And yet he was both an important innovator himself and an energetic promoter of the innovations of others, not only the first important champion of Cubism but a friend to every important painter of the time. Like the young Ezra Pound, he was extraordinarily generous to other poets and artists. His importance in the artistic life of pre-war Paris is revealed particularly vividly by the numerous fine drawings and paintings of him: by Braque, de Chirico, Max Jacob, Marie Laurencin, Picasso, Henri Rousseau, de Vlaminck and others.

Apollinaire's most striking characteristic is probably his openness. It is not so much that he was torn between the claims of the new and the old;[2] it is more that he was unusually open to *all* literary and artistic possibilities. While notorious for his rejection of punctuation and his *calligrams*, the visually inventive arrangements of words that are a precursor of concrete poetry, Apollinaire also wrote Whitmanesque free verse, delicate octosyllabics, discursive rhyming poetry, and even Alexandrines as resonant as Racine's. The variety of his subject matter and his range of emotional tone are no less striking: his readiness to embrace different techniques parallels an unusual degree of openness to experience. More than most writers, Apollinaire had the courage to give himself to a thought, feeling or image and follow it however far, and in whatever direction, it might lead him.

I have myself only recently come to know Apollinaire well. For many years I knew only 'Le Pont Mirabeau' and 'The Pretty

Redhead' – two poems I still see as the best introduction to his work. The former, his most famous early poem, is one of the most musical poems in the French language. The lines 'Comme la vie est lente / Et comme l'Espérance est violente' (literally: 'How slow life is / And how violent hope is') are witty and graceful and this outburst of impatience is all the more striking for occurring in a poem whose prevailing mood is one of nostalgia. 'The Pretty Redhead', written not long before Apollinaire's death, is both a love song and a poetic testament. The simplicity of the last lines is especially touching: 'But laugh laugh at me / Men everywhere especially people here / For there are so many things I'm afraid to tell you / So many things you'd never let me tell you / Have pity on me'. Like 'Le Pont Mirabeau', this poem reveals a vulnerability which is part of what makes Apollinaire so very approachable, more so than any other major French poet of the past century.

The next poem of Apollinaire's to impress me was a war poem, 'Wonder of the War'. This was unlike anything I had ever read. Apollinaire's ecstatic description of the beauty of a night sky lit up by flares and shell-fire is entirely convincing, but can be deeply shocking, especially to a reader who – like me at the time – expects all war poetry to be like Wilfred Owen's. I now see this poem as a supreme example of Apollinaire's ability to give free rein to his imagination without ever losing touch with reality. What shocks is simply the vividness with which he registers a painful truth: that beauty and violence can live side by side. The battlefield did indeed have its moments of beauty and – as Norma Rinsler has pointed out in her fine article on Apollinaire's war poetry[3] – Apollinaire is not the only writer to have registered this. Wyndham Lewis, for example, has written of the 'great romantic effects' of a night bombardment,[4] and the French writer Henri Ghéon described the night sky over the battlefield as 'the dance of night and the festival of speaking fire'.[5]

The first poems of Apollinaire's that I translated were 'Le Pont Mirabeau' and a selection from his delightful *Bestiary*, but it was my admiration of the war poems that impelled me to undertake this volume. These poems are still underrated – even in France. And while many poems from *Alcohols* – even quite slight ones – have been translated into English five or six times, most of the poems from *Calligrams* have only been translated once, and the posthumous collections, *Poems to Lou* and *Poems to Madeleine*, seem hardly to have been translated at all. Chronologically, the war poems fall into three groups: those written while Apollinaire was undergoing training in Nîmes, those written while he served in the artillery, and – a smaller group – those written while he served in the infantry. The poems in the first group are exuberant; though their optimism now seems naïve, they retain the power to move us. Apollinaire's excitement was shared by millions of people, and it is expressed vividly. Unlike much patriotic poetry, Apollinaire's never dissolves into abstraction; poems such as 'At Nîmes' are full of precisely observed detail.

The poems in the second group are imbued with wonder, excitement and eroticism. Many were first addressed either to Louise de Coligny ('Lou'), with whom Apollinaire had a passionate affair around the time he enlisted, or to Madeleine Pagès, whom Apollinaire met in early 1915 and to whom he became engaged. Some were sent simultaneously to both women. For all their apparent high-spiritedness, it would be inaccurate to call these poems escapist. Firstly, Apollinaire is extremely clear-minded about his wish to escape. One of his poems to Madeleine ends with the lines:

> Are you a goddess like the goddesses the Greeks created so as to feel less down-hearted
> I worship you O my exquisite goddess even if you live only in my imagination

Secondly, much of the imagery of even the most wildly erotic poems is derived from the immediate reality of the war. It is as if Apollinaire would like to retreat into sexual fantasy, but is prevented from doing so by the pressure of his day-to-day experience. The intensity of his desire to escape testifies to the depth of the horror he feels.

During his first six months of active service, Apollinaire was a gunner, positioned some way behind the front line and thus sheltered from the war's worst horrors. In November 1915 he asked to be transferred to the infantry. After this transfer he wrote of 'the front line trench whose horror can't be described, let alone imagined'.[6] And in December 1915, in a letter to Madeleine, he wrote: 'Imagine to what extent one is deprived in trench life of everything that joins you to the universe. One is simply a breast offering itself to the enemy.' Life in the artillery now seemed like 'a country picnic, an excursion whose risks aren't much greater than those of mountaineering.'[7] The mood of the later poems in *Calligrams* is correspondingly grimmer. There are still grimmer fragments that Apollinaire seems uncharacteristically to have kept to himself, perhaps afraid that his readers would not know what he was talking about. The following lines, for example, were not published during his lifetime:

> Harden yourself old heart hear the piercing cries
> Let out by the wounded in agony in the distance
> Men lice of the earth O tenacious vermin

The longer poems in *Calligrams* are remarkable for their imagery, for their visionary power. Many of the short lyrics in *Alcohols* are remarkable for the subtlety of their music. It was only while compiling this volume that I became aware of the power and depth of a group of apparently simple poems where Apollinaire's musical, painterly and intellectual gifts are fused: the short lyrics in *Calligrams*. I shall finish with a few reflections on 'Exercise', the poem Apollinaire chose to place immediately after 'Wonder of the War', no doubt seeing the depressive truthfulness of 'Exercise' as a corrective to the ecstasy of 'Wonder of the War'.

Norma Rinsler has written with regard to the later war poems: 'The early optimism about a better future was gone. The only way to avoid fear was not to think of the future at all.' She continues: 'In "Exercise" Apollinaire shows how this attitude detaches a man from life, so that the presence of death becomes less alien. His infantry men, like Wyndham Lewis's, hardly notice the shells; like monks they have trained themselves to the patient rhythm of an ascetic life which expects nothing of this world, and thus is not afraid of leaving it.'[8] Wyndham Lewis also served in the artillery and Norma Rinsler is referring here to a passage from his autobiography:

> More German batteries were firing now, and a number of shells intercepted us. We met an infantry party coming up, about ten men, with earthen faces and heads bowed, their eyes turned inwards as it seemed, to shut out this too-familiar scene. As a shell came rushing down beside them, they did not notice it. There was no sidestepping death if this was where you *lived*. It was worth *our* while to prostrate

> ourselves, when death came over-near. We might escape, *in spite of* death. But *they* were its servants. Death would not tolerate that optimistic obeisance from them![9]

The coincidence between this passage and Apollinaire's poem is remarkable:

> They quietly spoke of other years
> And gazed at the vast plain ahead
> A shell coughed near the bombardiers
> Not one so much as turned his head
>
> They only talked of yesterday
> Tomorrow seemed a waste of breath
> They held to their ascetic way
> This constant discipline of death

Norma Rinsler remarks in a footnote[10] that Apollinaire's 'touch is lighter than Wilfred Owen's in "Greater Love" or Siegfried Sassoon's in "Glory of Women"'. This is indeed true but, as Rinsler then implies, his understanding of war is no less profound. And he records a broader range of emotional response to the war.

The original of 'Confession' is published in *Apollinaire: Poésies Libres*, ed. Jean-Jacques Pauvert; for all other poems I have followed the Pléiade edition. My intention has been to represent the best of Apollinaire. I have, however, omitted all but one of the calligrams – which are hard to reproduce in a small format – and several fine poems that depend on untranslatable puns. I have also omitted 'La Chanson du Mal-Aimé', a poem I find monotonous. I am delighted to be able to include translations and original poems by so many fine poets. I regret that it has been impossible to include Samuel Beckett's version of 'Zone'.

Some translators scrupulously avoid looking at the work of their predecessors. I find this surprising: in most fields ignorance of this kind is considered unacceptable. I am myself indebted to most previous translators of Apollinaire. Meredith's translation of *Alcools* (New York: Doubleday, 1964) is the best translation of the volume as a whole. Anne Hyde Greet's bilingual edition of *Calligrammes* would be worth buying for the notes alone. I have also learned much from Francis Steegmuller's compellingly readable biography *Apollinaire: Poet among the Painters* (Harmondsworth: Penguin 1973). Professor Norma Rinsler's attentive help has been especially valuable. My wife has helped me resolve many difficulties, as have Anne Berkeley, David Black, Angela Brewer, Lucy Chandler, Elizabeth Cook, Major-General P. B. Foster, Harry Guest, Martha Kapos, Angela Livingstone, David Mus, Aline Schulman, William Valk, Angela Williams and John Wareham.

Translations should not require long apologies. Here I shall say only that I have stayed close to the literal meaning of the free-verse poems, but have allowed myself more latitude with regard to poems in metre and rhyme. I have tried to stay close to Apollinaire's forms. My first drafts of 'Autumn' and 'The Lorelei', however, seemed ponderous. In the end I settled for octosyllables, even though Apollinaire uses a line of twelve syllables or more; my version of 'The Lorelei' perhaps sounds somewhat jauntier than the original.

ROBERT CHANDLER

References

1. André Billy, in his preface to *Poèmes: Apollinaire* (Paris: Livre de Poche, 1963).
2. Although this conflict is indeed the theme of 'La Jolie Rousse'.
3. 'The War Poems of Apollinaire' in *French Studies*, April 1971, p. 181.
4. *Blasting and Bombardiering* (London: John Calder, 1982), p. 116 (cited in 'The War Poems of Apollinaire').
5. *Foi en la France* (Paris, 1916), p. 77 (cited in 'The War Poems of Apollinaire').
6. Apollinaire, *Lettres à sa Marraine 1915–18*, ed. Adéma (Paris: 1951), p. 58.
7. Rouveyre, *Apollinaire* (Paris, 1945), p. 241.
8. Rinsler, 'The War Poems of Apollinaire', p. 177.
9. From Wyndham Lewis, *Blasting and Bombardiering*, pp. 135–6.
10. 'The War Poems of Apollinaire', p. 185.

Part One

Poems from *Bestiary*

Tortoise

From Thrace we have the mystic lyre,
Made by Hermes from a tortoise.
Mountain lions dance from their lair –
We sing as Orpheus taught us.

Kashmir Goat

Neither the curls that Jason dared
His life for, nor this goat's fine coat
Can be compared
With the gold curls that hold my heart ensnared.

Serpent

You've got it in for beauty.
Think of the women who have been
Victims of your cruelty –
Eve, Cleopatra, Eurydice,
And one or two others I've seen.

Lion

Unhappy image of our age
And the sad fall of royalty;
This one was born inside a cage
In Hamburg, by a chilly sea.

Mice

O mice of time, brief day by day,
You slyly gnaw my life away;
And all too soon I'll have misspent
Twenty-eight years, I'm sad to say.

Caterpillar

Work hard, poets, work with good cheer:
Work leads to wealth and freedom from fear;
And butterflies, for all their graces,
Are merely caterpillars who persevere.

Cricket

This is the slender cricket
Saint John once used to eat.
May my verses be like it –
And feed the true elite!

Dolphin

Dolphins leap through the air,
But the sea stays salt and bitter;
Dreams may burst into flower,
But life remains without pity.

Octopus

He clouds the world with ink
And likes to drink
His loved ones' blood.
I'm similar, I think.

Jellyfish

Floppy heads
Violet hair-do –
But they enjoy a tempest
As much as I do.

Crayfish

My mind is never quite made up
And changing it brings me delight.
I move through life much like a crayfish,
This way, that way, never straight.

Louse

We can learn resolve from this insect
We deem so low;
Scratch, gentlemen, to your hearts' content –
He won't let go.

Carp

You live longer than we do
In your lake in the park.
Has Death forgotten you,
O melancholy carp?

Peacock

Often he trails his tail on the grass
But, when he's feeling randier,
He shows it off in all its grandeur –
And so displays his arse.

Ibis

Bird of the Nile, bird of dread,
Your Latin name is like a knell,
Reminding me: 'You too shall dwell
In the pale kingdom of the dead.'

Part Two

Alcohols and Other Pre-War Poems

Le Pont Mirabeau

Beneath the Pont Mirabeau flows the Seine
And our love too
Must I live through it all again
Joy always followed in the wake of pain

Let night come on   bells end the day
Days pass by   I stay

Stretch out your hands to me   and meet my eyes
There lies the Seine
Beneath our bridge of arms she lies
Deep river that has heard so many sighs

Let night come on   bells end the day
Days pass by   I stay

Love slips away   the river sings this song
Love slips away
Life is so slow   life is lifelong
And hope is so hot-headed   so headstrong

Let night come on   bells end the day
Days pass by   I stay

Days pass   weeks pass   all to the same refrain
Neither time past
Nor loves will come this way again
Beneath the Pont Mirabeau flows the Seine

Let night come on   bells end the day
Days pass by   I stay

Le Pont Mirabeau

(for Peter Josyph)

Beneath the Pont Mirabeau flows the Seine
And then our loves
Must I recall again
Joy only ever happened after pain

Let the hour chime night arrive
Days go by I stay alive

Hands clasped let's look each other in the eye
While through the bridge
Formed by our arms glides by
The river weary of long scrutiny

Let the hour chime night arrive
Days go by I stay alive

Love goes away the way these waters flow
Love goes away
Living appears so slow
And hope can deal us such a violent blow

Let the hour chime night arrive
Days go by I stay alive

The days pass and the weeks pass all in vain
Neither time past
Nor love returns again
Beneath the Pont Mirabeau flows the Seine

Let the hour chime night arrive
Days go by I stay alive

(trans. Harry Guest)

Meadow Saffron

The meadow is poisonous but pretty in the fall
The cows that pasture there
Slowly become poisoned
Meadow saffron the colour of lilacs and of the skin around
  eyes
Flower there your eyes are like that flower
Bluish purple like the skin around them and like this fall
And for your eyes my life has slowly become poisoned

Kids out of school come noisily
Wearing jackets and playing mouth organs
They pick the meadow saffron which are like mothers
Daughters of their daughters and the colour of your eyelids
Fluttering as flowers flutter in a mad wind

The guardian of the herd sings softly
As slowly the bellowing cows abandon
Forever this great meadow ill-flowered by the fall

(trans. D. M. Black)

Autumn Crocus

The field's poisonous but pretty on autumn days
The cows eat a slow
Poison as they graze
The autumn crocus flowers there its lilac shadow lies
In circles like the circle of your eyes
Mauve as circling shadows or the sick year
And my life for your eyes' poison slowly dies

Mouth organs blare Here come the loud kids
In crumpled jackets fresh out of school they bend
To pick the autumn crocus that are mothers
Daughters of their daughters and your shadowed lids
That flutter as flowers flutter in the crazed wind

The cowherd sings out his soft phrase
As lowing now the heavy cows no longer graze
Leaving for ever this great field full
Of bitter flowers to the sun's thin rays

(trans. Susan Wicks)

Dusk

On a lawn where daylight fades
Brushed by shadows and by shades
Columbine lies by the pool
Sees her flesh so white and cool

A showman all in twilight grey
Lists the wonders they'll enact
The sky is colourless and pricked
With stars as pale as whey

Harlequin then leaps on stage
Waves his greetings to the girls
Welcomes fairies and a mage
Versed in old Bohemian spells

Plucking stars down from the night
He juggles them with outstretched hand
While a man who's just been hanged
Plays the cymbals with his feet

A blind young woman rocks her son
A roe-deer passes with her fawn

A dwarf has cast an envious look
At Hermes-Pierrot of the Book

Annie

On the Texas coast
Between Mobile and Galveston
A big garden overflows
With roses, and it holds a house
Itself a large rose.

A lady takes a stroll at times
All alone among her plants
And when I pass her on her avenue of limes
We exchange a glance.

The sect she follows bears the name
Of Mennonite. No buttons on her clothes,
No buds between her roses' leaves.
There are two missing from my sleeves.
The lady's sacred practices and mine are almost the same.

(trans. Susan Wicks)

The House of the Dead

(for Maurice Reynal)

Stretching over the grassy slopes
The house of the dead
Framed the cemetery like a cloister
Its windows

Were like the windows of smart shops
Though the mannequins inside
Were not standing up
But lying down and grinning for eternity

After two or three weeks in Munich
I happened for the first time
Upon this almost deserted cemetery
And my teeth chattered at the sight
Of so much bourgeoisie
Laid out in their finery
And waiting to be buried

Suddenly
Instant as my memory
Eyes lit up again
In one glass cell after another
A lively apocalypse
Filled the sky with people
And the now pre-Galilean
And infinitely flat earth
Was covered by a thousand unchanging mythologies
A diamond angel shattered all the windows
And the dead greeted me
With otherworldly looks
But their faces and their bearing
Soon became less funereal
And earth and sky lost
Their phantasmagoric air

The dead were delighted to see
Their departed bodies
Between them and the light
They laughed at their shadows
And studied them
As if they were
The lives they'd left behind

Then I counted them up
There were forty-nine men

Women and children
Visibly growing more beautiful
And now watching me
With so much warmth
Even tenderness
That I suddenly took to them
And asked if they'd like
To come for a walk with me
Far from the arcades of their house

And we left the cemetery
All together arm in arm
Humming military airs
Now that sin has been disarmed

We crossed the city
Often meeting friends
And relatives who joined
Our little company of the newly dead
Everyone was so bright
So charming so healthy
You'd need to have been very smart
To tell the dead from the living

In the countryside
We spread out
Two cavalrymen joined us
And were made welcome
They cut shoots of elder
And viburnum
Made them into whistles
And gave them to the children

Later there was partying in the open air
Putting their hands on one another's shoulders
Couples danced to the shrill sound of zithers

They hadn't forgotten how to dance
These dead men and dead women
They knew how to drink too

Now and again a bell
Tolled that a new cask
Was about to be broached

A dead woman sitting on a bench
By a barberry bush
Let a young student
Kneel at her feet
And propose marriage

I shall wait ten years for you
Twenty years if need be
Your wish shall be my wish

I shall wait for you
All your life
Said the dead woman

Some children
From this world or maybe the next
Sang a few of those rounds
With senseless and lyrical words
That must be all that's left
Of humanity's
Most ancient poetical monuments

The student slipped a ring
Onto the dead girl's finger
Here is the pledge of my love
Of our betrothal
Neither time nor absence
Will make us forget our promises
And one day we shall have a fine wedding
With sprigs of myrtle
On our clothes and in your hair
A fine sermon in church
Long speeches after the feast
And music
Music

Our children
Said the fiancée
Will be finer still finer
(Alas! the ring was broken)
Than if they were made of silver or gold
Than if they were emerald or diamond
They will be brighter still brighter
Than the stars of the firmament
Than the light of the dawn
Than your eyes my betrothed
They will smell even sweeter
(Alas! the ring was broken)
Than lilac that has just blossomed
Than thyme or a rose or a sprig
Of lavender or rosemary
The musicians went on their way
And we continued our walk

On the shore of a lake
We stopped to play ducks and drakes
Spinning flat stones
Across water that was almost still

We came to a harbour
Where some boats were tied up
Once all of us were on board
We pushed off
And some of the dead
Put their backs into it
And swung their oars just like the living

In the bows of the boat I was steering
A dead man was talking to a young woman
Wearing a yellow dress
A black bodice with blue ribbons
And a grey hat
Trimmed with a single limp feather

I love you
He said

As a cock pigeon loves his hen
As a night moth
Loves the light

Too late
Replied the living woman
Cast aside cast aside your forbidden love
I'm a married woman
Look at my shining ring
My hands are trembling
I'm crying I want to die

The boats had now reached
A place where the cavalrymen
Knew that an echo answered from the shore
We could have questioned it for evermore
And our questions were so extravagant
And the answers so very pertinent
We could have died of laughing
And the dead man said to the living woman

Together we would be so happy
The water will close over us
But you're crying and your hands are trembling
Neither of us need walk the earth again

We made land then set off back home
Beautiful-mouthed couples
Sauntered along at their own pace
And continued their courting
The dead men had chosen living women
And the living men – dead women
An occasional juniper
Resembled a ghost

The children rent the air
As they blew hollow-cheeked
On their whistles made from elder
Or viburnum
While the soldiers sang Tyrolean songs

Answering one another
As they do in the high mountains

Back in town
Our band grew slowly smaller
People said
Goodbye
So long
See you tomorrow
Quite a few of them went into cafés
Some left us
By a shop that sells dog-meat
And went in to buy their evening meal

Soon I was on my own with the dead
Who kept straight on
To the cemetery
And
There they were again
Beneath the arcades
Motionless
Correctly dressed
Lying behind glass
And waiting to be buried

They had no idea
About what had happened
But the living remembered it
As an unhoped-for happiness
That was so real
They had no fear of losing it

And they lived their lives so nobly
That people who the day before
Had looked on them as equals
Or even somewhat less than equals
Now admired
Their power their wealth their genius
For nothing can be so elevating
As to have loved a dead man or woman

You become so pure you end up
United
In the glaciers of memory
With what you remember
You are strengthened for life
And no longer need anyone

from Cortège

One day
One day as I was waiting for myself
I said to myself Guillaume it's time you showed up
So I can finally know just who I am
I know other people
I know them by my five senses and by a few others besides
It's enough for me to see their feet and I can reconstruct these people
It's enough for me to see their frightened feet a single hair of their heads
Or their tongues when I feel like playing doctor
Or their children when I feel like playing prophet
The vessels of ship owners the pens of my colleagues
The loose change of a blind man the hands of a mute
Or a letter written by anyone over the age of twenty
And I mean not from the handwriting but from the choice of words
It's enough for me to smell the insides of their churches
The rivers in their cities
The flowers in public gardens
O Cornelius Agrippa the smell of one little dog would have enabled me
To give an exact description of the citizens of Cologne
Their magi kings and the Ursuline swarm
That inspired your error regarding all women
The taste of a laurel leaf from the garden is enough to make me fall in love or start to mock

And I can be quite certain from touching someone's clothes
whether or not they feel the cold
O the people I know
It's enough for me to hear their footsteps
To be able to point out for all time which way they have
gone
And all this makes me feel I have the right
To bring other people to life
And so one day I was waiting for myself
Guillaume I said to myself it's time you showed up
And those I love drew near with lyric step
But I wasn't there
Giants covered in seaweed moved through their cities
Beneath the sea where only the towers were islands
And with the clarities of its depths
This sea flowed in my veins and made my heart beat
Then a thousand white tribes appeared on the earth
And each man held a rose in his hand
And the language they made up as they walked
Is the one I learned from their mouths and still speak

The cortège passed I looked for my own body
And all the people there who were not me
Brought one by one small pieces of myself
And slowly built me as you build a tower
Millions heaped themselves up and I was formed
From all these bodies all these human things

You past You dead You gods who fashioned me
I'm just like you I only live in passing
Turning my eyes away from the blank future
I see how all the past still grows within me

Nothing is dead but what has not been born
Tomorrow is pale beside the shining past
Beside such perfect energy and form
Tomorrow's nothing but an empty waste

Marie

You danced there when you were quite small
Will you still dance there when you're old
They prance and caper at the ball
One day the bells will all have tolled
Marie won't you come back at all

The masks we wear are so discreet
The music seems as far away
As where the sky and skyline meet
Ah yes I'll love you but in a half-hearted way
And what is wrong with me is sweet

The flocks set off into the snow
Those flakes of silver flecks of wool
Some soldiers pass why can't I show
A heart I own not one that's cool
Then warm and yet what do I know

Do I know why your hair will fade
That curls now like an angry sea
Do I know why your hair will fade
Like leaves along the autumn we
Have littered with the vows we made

I used to walk along the Seine
An old book underneath my arm
The river is so like my pain
It flows unquenchable and calm
When will the weekend come again

(trans. Harry Guest)

Poem Read at the Wedding of André Salmon

(13 July 1909)

Seeing this morning's flags I didn't say to myself:
Look at the rich garments of the poor
Or democratic modesty is veiling its grief from me
Or so as to honour liberty we copy the leaves of trees
(O vegetable Liberty O sole Liberty on earth)
Or houses are on fire because people are leaving never to return
Or tomorrow these restless hands will be working for all of us
Or even people who didn't know what to do with life have been hung
Or even people are re-forming the world by re-storming the Bastille
I know no one will reform the world unless he is rooted in poetry
And that Paris is decked out in flags because my friend André Salmon is getting married there

We met in some accursed
Cellar when we were young
We were both smoking and waiting for the dawn in threadbare clothes
Spellbound spellbound by the same words whose meaning needs to be changed
Young men who'd got it wrong all wrong and had yet to learn how to laugh
The table and the two glasses gazed at us like a dying Orpheus
The glasses fell and shattered
And we learned how to laugh
Then we set off pilgrims of perdition
Across streets across countries across reason

I saw him next on the bank of the river where Ophelia was floating
And still floats white among the lilies
He disappeared among pale Hamlets
Playing tunes of madness on a flute
And then I saw him reciting the beatitudes beside a dying *moujik*
And admiring snow that was like naked women
I saw him doing this or that in honour of the same words
That change the faces of children and I'm saying all this
Saying what has been and what will be because my friend André Salmon is getting married

Let us rejoice not because our friendship has been the river which has made us fecund
Fertile plains whose abundance is the food we all hope for
Nor because our wine glasses are once more gazing at us like a dying Orpheus
Nor because we have grown so much that our eyes could be mistaken for stars
Nor because these flags are flying outside the windows of citizens who for a hundred years have been glad to be alive and to have little things to defend
Nor because we are rooted in poetry and have rights over the words that make and unmake the universe
Nor because we can cry without looking stupid yet know how to laugh
Nor because we are smoking and drinking as in the old days
Let us rejoice because the conductor of poets and of fire
The love which like light
Fills all the solid space between the stars and planets
Love orders my friend André Salmon to get married today

The Parting

I've picked a sprig of heather
Autumn's dead don't forget
We'll never meet again and yet
Scent of time sprig of heather
I'm still waiting don't forget

Mountebanks

A troop of acrobats and clowns
Is trailing through the dusty plain
Past empty hamlets and grey inns
Past garden walls and fields of grain

The children seem to know no fear
Their elders walk behind and dream
Apple and pear will be stripped bare
Should this troop catch sight of them

They carry weights of every shape
And gilded hoops and hefty drums
While two wise friends a bear an ape
Stretch out a bowl and beg for alms

The Gypsy Woman

Our nights would darken our days
The old gypsy knew all along
We thanked her and went on our way
Hoping to prove her wrong

Love danced when we were together
Danced about like a circus bear
The bluebird dropped her feathers
And beggars forgot their prayer

We can stray but not from our fate
Yet our hope to find love on the way
Makes us try hand in hand to forget
What we heard the old gypsy say

Autumn

A knock-kneed peasant and his ox
Pass slowly by through autumn fog
That hides the down-at-heel farms

And as he plods along he hums
A song of love and love forsaken
A song of how a heart is broken

The summer has now breathed her last
Grey figures slip through rings of mist

Autumn

Hirplan[1] throu haar[2] see thon shacht[3] fairmer wi a stirk[4]
Daunneran[5] by gey[6] slaw in the October haar
That haps[7] the plewmen's puir slummy fairm-touns wi mirk

And gangan on his wey the fairmer croons afaur
A ballant of tined[8] luve and luve's ill-keepit traist
That tells about a ring and a hairt brast for wae

Oh! autumn the autumn has laid the simmer waste
Intill the haar thae twa muve silhouettit grey

(trans. Robert Garioch)

1 limping
2 mist
3 lame
4 bullock
5 strolling
6 very
7 covers
8 lost

from The Brazier

To the noble fire that I adore
And carry with me I have fed
Live hands and even this Past (God rest
Its soul) these heads of the dead
Flame I do what you desire

The sudden gallop of the stars
Is only the course of things to come
One with the hungry mating cries
Of centaurs whinnying at stud
And the old lament of trees

Where have my many faces gone
The God I worshipped as a child
Love has now turned sly and mean
Let the new tongues flare again
My soul is stripping in the sun

The plain is forested with flames
We've hung our hearts from lemon trees
The severed heads that shout acclaim
Those heavenly bodies that wept blood
Are only heads with women's names

The river fastened on the town
Pins you in place like a clout
And so a slave to Amphion's sweet sound
You suffer each beguiling tone
That turns a stone to mountain goat

(trans. Susan Wicks)

Rhenish Night

My glass is filled with a wine that trembles like flame.
Listen, a boatman is singing a slow song
About a moonlit night when seven women came
Out of the river and their hair was green and long.

Now sing and dance until the terrace whirls
And the boatman's slow song fades
And bring me all the pretty blond-haired girls
With the still gaze and the coiled braids.

The Rhine flows drunk, its vine-leaves trailing after,
The trembling gold of night is mirrored there.
Like a death rattle the slow song grows softer
About the nymphs who bewitched the summer with their green hair –

My glass has shattered like a peal of laughter.

(trans. William Meredith)

The Lorelei

She was a sorceress and blonde
She made men mad she made men blind

The bishop called her to be tried
But then decreed she must be freed

O Lorelei your eyes are jewels
Who taught your eyes to cast such spells

My eyes are cursed my heart is tired
One glance at me and men have died

My eyes aren't jewels my eyes are flames
Their sorcery must be condemned

Their fire burns me O Lorelei
Let someone else send you to die

O reverend bishop please don't joke
My soul needs prayers my flesh the stake

My love has gone he won't return
Since I can't love please let me burn

If you refuse why then my eyes
My cruel eyes must end my days

My love has gone I am bereft
My heart it hurts my love has left

The priest he summoned three bold knights
Take her he said to be God's bride

Live in God's house O Lorelei
Die to the world yet do not die

The four set off towards the river
Her eyes like stars she begged this favour

Sirs these fine lands were once my own
So let me climb to that high stone

And let me gaze into the Rhine
And see my face for one last time

And let me look on flowers and meadows
Before I join young girls and widows

Her curls were sunbeams in the wind
The watching knights were all struck blind

A boat is sailing down the river
And on the boat I see my lover

And my heart melts at my love's cry
She leans she falls into the Rhine

The Rhine shall be her bed for ever
She's seen her eyes in the clear river

Fir Trees

The firs, like old astrologers
In robes and pointed cowls, incline
Their tops to fallen brother firs
That move as boats along the Rhine.

Schooled by their elders the great poets
In the seven arts, the firs divine
That some day, brighter than the planets
Their destiny will be to shine,

But softly shine, as old stars glow,
When happy Christmastimes arouse
The dreaming firs adrift with snow,
Nodding their long and languorous boughs.

The autumn night makes them musicians
Who teach the wind forgotten numbers;
At other times as grave magicians
They charm the sky until it thunders.

In winter, flights of cherubim
Replace them, fluttering in repose;
Summertime makes rabbis of them
Or old maids wearing somber clothes.

Wandering doctors with sweet salves,
They ease the mountain's labor pain;
From time to time an old fir heaves
And lies down in the hurricane.

(trans. William Meredith)

The Lady

Rap rap His door is shut
The lilies in his garden past their best
Who *is* this corpse they're carting out

You've just been knocking at his house
And scuttle scuttle
scuttle goes the little mouse

(trans. Susan Wicks)

from *The Betrothals*

Forgive me my ignorance
Forgive me for no longer knowing the ancient game of versifying
I no longer know anything and I love uniquely
The flowers in my eyes become flame again
Divinely I meditate
And I smile at all the beings I have not created
But if the time should come when shadow solid at last
Could multiply itself and realize the formal diversity of my love
I would delight in my handiwork

(trans. D. M. Black)

1909

The lady was wearing a dress
Of violet-coloured silk
And her gold-embroidered tunic
Was made up of two panels
Fastened at the shoulder

Her eyes dancing like angels
She laughed she laughed
She had a face the colours of France
Blue eyes white teeth and very red lips
She had a face the colours of France

Her dress had a low round neck
Her hair was styled like Récamier's
Her fine arms were bare

Will we never hear midnight strike

The lady in the embroidered tunic
And the violet dress
With the low round neck
Was parading her curls
Her gold headband
Scuffing her little buckled shoes

She was so beautiful
You'd never have dared to love her

I loved ghastly women in monstrous districts
Where new creatures are born every day
Iron their blood their brains flame
I loved I loved the skilled race of machines
Luxury and beauty are only their froth
That woman was so beautiful
She scared me

Inside

I

I have to strip right to the skin
They lead me to a cell
Guillaume what have you gone and done
I hear a strange voice wail

I've walked alive into a grave
Lazarus in reverse
Farewell *jeunes filles* farewell my years
Of song and wine and verse

II

I'm not Guillaume or Guy
        In this cell
I'm section fifteen
        Number twelve

Rays of sun infiltrate
        Dusty panes
Silent clowns that have lit
        On these lines

As I watch I can hear
        The slow tread
Of my fellow in the cell
        Overhead

III

Mornings I go for a walk
Like a bear in a pen
There and back   there and back
The sky is blue as a chain
Mornings I go for a walk
Like a bear in a pen

In the cell next to mine
Someone turns on a tap
Let guards pace up and down
Clinking keys with each step
In the cell next to mine
Someone turns on a tap

IV

I feel so sad between the naked walls
    Of this pale cell of mine
A fly takes little steps across the page
    Perusing these unequal lines

What will become of me O God you know my sorrow
    You gave it me and brought me here
Pity my tearless eyes pity this pale body
    The creaking of my shackled chair

Pity each poor heart beating in this prison
    And Love who walks beside me
Pity above all my now so feeble reason
    And the despair that blinds me

V

How slowly the hours pass
Like a funeral passing by

You will mourn this hour of mourning
Which will pass too fast
As all hours pass

VI

Sounds of city life pass by
A prisoner has no horizon
All I see is a hostile sky
The bare walls of my prison

Day is over a lamp is lit
A lamp is lit in my prison

We two are alone tonight
Sweet clarity Dear reason

Prayer

When I was little
My mother always dressed me in blue and white
O Holy Virgin
Do you still love me
For my part I
Know very well that I
Shall love you till I die
Except that really it's all over
I no longer believe in heaven or hell
I no longer believe I no longer believe
The sailor who was rescued
For always remembering
His daily Hail Mary
Looked like me looked like me

(trans. Richard Price and Robert Chandler)

The Confession

Last Maundy Thursday, Madame Marinée,
Who was just eighty,
Went to confess, to escape damnation.
She spoke first of this and that,
Then slipped in: 'Alas, my Father, I have made
Love!' 'Love!' said the father,
'In spite of your cold years?
When was the last time?'

'When I was twenty,'
Replied the old lady.
'Heavens!' said the priest. 'Why tell me that?
Or have you not confessed since then?'
'I confess each year, my father.'
'Why then tell me
Of a sixty-year-old sin?'
'I have a young soul in an old body,
Father. I love to remember my fine sin.'

Inscription for the Tomb of the Painter Henri Rousseau the Customs Inspector

Dear Rousseau I know you can hear us
Greetings
From Delaunay his wife Monsieur Queval and me
Let our luggage in duty-free through heaven's gate
And we'll bring you brushes and colours and canvases
So you can devote your holy leisure in the true light
To painting not my portrait this time
But the face of the stars

The Windows

From red to green all the yellow is dying
When macaws sing in their native forests
Entrails of pihis
There's a poem to be written about that one-winged bird
We'll send it by telephone
Monstrous state of shock
It makes your eyes run
See that pretty young girl in the crowd of young Turinaises

The poor young man blew his nose on his white tie
You will raise the curtain
Now watch the window open
Spiders when light was woven by hands
Beauty paleness unfathomable violets
We shall try vainly to get some rest
It will start at midnight
When you have time you have freedom
Winkles Devilfish multiple Suns and the sunset's Sea-Urchin
An old pair of yellow shoes in front of the window
Towers
Towers are streets
Wells
Wells are squares
Wells
Hollow trees shelter homeless mulatto girls
The Chabins sing sad songs of dying
To brown Chabines
And the goose trumpets waa-waa to the north
Where racoon-hunters
Scrape skins
Sparkling diamond
Vancouver
Where the train white with snow and its nightlights runs
  away from winter
O Paris
From red to green all the yellow is dying
Paris Vancouver Hyères Maintenon New York and the
  West Indies
The window opens like an orange
Light's beautiful fruit

(trans. John Wareham and Robert Chandler)

Monday on Christine Street

The concierge and the concierge's mother will turn a blind eye
If you're any sort of a man you'll come with me tonight
We just need one bloke to watch the main entrance
While someone else goes upstairs

Three gas lights burning
The woman who owns the place has TB
When you're through we can have a game of backgammon
A band-leader with a sore throat
In Tunis we'll get you to smoke some dope

Sounds good to me

Piles of saucers flowers a calendar
Bim bam bim
I owe the landlady damn near three hundred francs
I'd sooner cut off my you know what than let her have them

I'm leaving at 8:27
Six mirrors staring each other out
I think we're getting into even more of a pickle
My dear sir
To me you're no more than a breadcrumb
That woman's got a nose like a tapeworm
Louise has forgotten her fur
Well I haven't got a fur and I don't feel the least bit cold
The Dane smokes a cigarette as he studies the timetable
The black cat walks right through the restaurant

Those pancakes were divine
The tap's running
Dress black as her nails
That's utterly impossible
Here you are sir
The malachite ring

The floor's sprinkled with sawdust
It's true then
The redheaded waitress has run off with a bookseller

A journalist I really scarcely know

Listen Jacques I've got something very serious to tell you

A mixed shipping company

Then he says to me sir would you care to see what I can do
in the way of etchings and pictures
I've only got one little maid

After lunch at the Café du Luxembourg
The moment we get there he introduces me to this hefty feller
Who says
Hey that's charming
Smyrna Naples Tunisia
Where the hell's it gone
Last time I was in China
That's eight or nine years ago
Honour often depends on the swing of the pendulum
The time on the clock face
A royal flush

Hotel

My room's shaped like a cage
The sun slips a hand through the window
But I just want to smoke and dream
I light up from the light of day
Don't want to work
I want to smoke

Teacher's Daydream

My classroom is a cage the sun
sticks an arm right through the bars
so handy for lighting little cigars
these French lessons are a joke
I don't want to teach I want to smoke

(Christopher Reid)

On Prophecies

I've known several lady prophets
Madame Salmajour had learned in Oceania to tell fortunes
from cards
She had also had the chance there to take part
In a tasty little evening of cannibalism
Something she didn't talk about to just anyone
Concerning the future she was never wrong

A Ceretanian fortune-teller Marguerite something-or-other
Is equally skilled
But Madame Deroy is the most inspired
The most exact
Everything she's told me about the past has been true and
everything
She's predicted has come true when she said it would
I knew a sciomancer but I didn't want him interrogating my
shadow
I know a water diviner Diriks the Norwegian painter

Broken mirror spilt salt or bread dropped on the ground
May these faceless gods always spare me
All the same I don't believe but I look and I listen and please
note

That I'm not a bad reader of palms myself
Because I don't believe but I look and when possible I listen

Everyone is a prophet my dear André Billy
But people have been led for so long to believe
That they have no future and will never know anything
And are born idiots
That they have grown resigned and none of them even thinks
Of wondering whether or not he knows the future
There's nothing religious about any of this
Neither in superstitions nor in prophecies
Nor in all that is called occultism
There is above all a way of observing nature
And of interpreting nature
That is entirely legitimate

A Phantom of Cloud

Around four in the afternoon
It being the fourteenth of July the next day
I went out onto the street to see the tumblers

People doing turns in the open
Are getting scarce in Paris
There were more of them around when I was young
Now they've nearly all left the city

I took the Boulevard Saint-Germain
And in a little square between Saint-Germain-des-Prés and the statue of Danton
I found the tumblers

The crowd round about them was silent and patient
I found myself a place in the circle so I could see
Formidable weights

Belgian cities lifted into the air by the outstretched arms of a
Russian worker from Longwy
Hollow black dumb-bells whose shaft is a frozen river
Fingers rolling a cigarette as delicious and bitter as life

The ground was covered with dirty rugs
Rugs with creases that can never be smoothed
Rugs almost entirely the colour of dust
With a few of those yellow or green stains that are as
persistent
As a tune you can't get out of your head

Can you see that thin wild-looking character
His greying beard was his ancestors' ashes seeping out from
inside him
The whole of his heredity was displayed on his face
He seemed to be dreaming of the future
As he mechanically turned a barrel-organ
Whose leisurely voice was a wondrous lament
All gurgles, squawks and smothered groans

The tumblers didn't move
The eldest wore an outfit that was the same livid pink as the
cheeks of those young women who seem full of life but are
close to death

That pink nests most of all in the creases that often surround
their mouths
Or near the base of their nostrils
It's a treacherous pink

And so this man wore on his back
The vile colour of his own lungs

Everywhere there were arms
Hands and arms mounting guard

The second tumbler
Had nothing on but his shadow
I watched him for a long time

His face quite escapes me
He's a man with no head

Another would have looked like an apache
A splendidly disgraceful young villain
What with his baggy trousers and garters to hold up his socks
Only he looked more like a pimp getting dressed

The music went silent and there was a lot of argie-bargie with the public
Sou by sou they threw onto the rug the sum of two francs fifty
Instead of the three francs the old man had declared was the price of the show
But when it became clear that no one was going to give any more
They decided to start the performance
From beneath the organ there emerged a very small acrobat got up in pulmonary pink
With fur round his wrists and his ankles
Uttering brief cries
He spread his fore-arms in a gracious
And open-handed salutation

One leg behind him ready to kneel
He saluted the four points of the compass
But when he walked on a ball
His slim body turned into such delicate music that not one of his audience was unmoved
A tiny spirit free of anything human
So each of us felt
And this music of forms
Overwhelmed the music of the mechanical organ
Being ground by the man whose face was covered with ancestors

The little acrobat did a cartwheel
With such harmony
That the organ stopped playing

And the organist hid his face in his hands
His fingers were the image of his destined descendants
Miniature foetuses being born from his beard
Then more Redskin war-cries
Angel music from the trees
And the child was gone

The tumblers lifted the great dumb-bells at arm's length
They juggled their weights
But each of the spectators was looking inside himself for the
  miraculous child
Century O century of cloud

Part Three

Poems Written 1914–18

The Little Car

On August 31 1914
I left Deauville shortly before midnight
In Rouveyre's little car

Counting the chauffeur there were three of us

We said farewell to a whole era
Furious giants were looming over Europe
Eagles left their eyries to wait for the sun
Voracious fish rose up from the depths
Whole nations were eager to know one another more deeply
And were rushing towards one another
The dead trembled with fear in their dark dwellings

The dogs were all barking at the frontiers
And I carried inside me all these armies that were fighting
I felt them rise up inside me I felt whole countries spread out
as the armies wound through them
Belgium's forests and happy villages
Francorchamps Eau Rouge and its springs
Always a favoured region for invasions
Railway arteries along which men on their way to die
Gave one last salute to life and its colours
Deep oceans where monsters were stirring
In old shipwrecked carcasses
Unimaginable heights where men fight
Higher than eagles soar
Man fights there against man
And falls suddenly like a shooting star

Within me I felt skilful new beings
Building and arranging a new universe
A merchant of unheard-of wealth and prodigious stature
Was laying out an extraordinary display of wares
And huge shepherds led

Great silent flocks that grazed on words
And were barked at by all the dogs on the road

I shall never forget that night journey during which none of us said a word
O dark departure with our three headlights dying
O tender night from before the war
O villages towards which blacksmiths summoned between midnight and one in the morning were hurriedly making their way
Not far from Lisieux the very blue or Versailles the golden
And we had to stop three times to change a burst tyre

And when after passing through Fontainebleau
In the afternoon
We arrived in Paris
Just as the mobilisation was being posted
My friend and I both understood
That the little car had driven us into a
New Era
And that although we were both mature men
We had only just been born

At Nîmes

(for Émile Léonard)

I enlisted under a deep blue sky
In Nice the city of Victory

One of nine hundred drivers I have no name
A carter in a new *Charroi de Nîmes*

Love told me to stay but I hear far-off shells
Ardently seeking and wedding their goals

I'm waiting for Spring to give the command
And send us greenhorns to fight for our land

Three gunners talking three heads converge
Their eyes are shining as bright as my spurs

A fine afternoon on guard at the stable
The call of the trumpets is bright and noble

I admire the gaiety of this detachment
We'll join our fine regiment up at the front

A reservist is munching anchovy and endive
As he tells me what's happened to his sick wife

Four gunners patiently work on their gun
One of them's stifling a curse or a moan

A spirit-level can be strangely perverse
The bubble rolls about like the eye of a horse

Girault's got a fine voice he sings after nine
An air from grand opera you can't help crying

With one hand I stroke our little grey gun
And think of grey Paris and the grey Seine

But in the canteen a wounded soldier
Talks of shells at night and their silver splendour

I slowly chew on my helping of meat
And walk on my own from five until eight

I saddle my horse and we scour the farms
I hail you from afar O great tower of Nîmes

XIV Because You Spoke to Me of Vice (from *Poems to Lou*)

You spoke to me of vice when you wrote yesterday
Vice has no part in sublime love
It's no more than a grain of sand in the sea
A single grain sinking into glassy abysses

We can call up imagination
Make our senses dance over the world's rubble
Wear ourselves out to the point of exasperation
Or wallow together in disgusting mud

And bound to each other by a unique pressure
We can defy death and its destiny
When our teeth chatter in chattering panic
We can call what is called morning evening

You can make a god of my wild whimsy
I can prostrate myself as if at an altar
Before your buttocks bloodied by my fury
Our love will remain pure as a pure sky

What does it matter that breathless dumb open-mouthed
Like two heavy cannon fallen from their emplacements
Broken with too much loving our bodies rest inert
Our love will always remain what it was

Let us ennoble the imagination my heart
Poor humanity all too often has so little of it
Vice in all that is no more than an illusion
Only coarse souls will ever be deceived by it

(trans. D. M. Black)

XXIII (from *Poems to Lou*)

Four days my love no letter still from you
The daylight's blotted out the sun gone blank
The barracks have become a place of terror
And I am sad as a transported horse

What's happened are you sad my love or tired
Or sick You said You promised you would write
Please fire your letter from your pen your gun
Let me have back my life and joie de vivre

Eight times I've asked the orderly and heard
'Nothing for you this time' And almost wept
I sought out in the street that pretty mongrel
That once we met together dearest heart

I stroked him gently and remembered you
I think he too remembered when we met
He licked my hand and looked at me with kindness
And he's the only friend I have in Nîmes

No news of you and I am in despair
What are you doing Will I hear tomorrow
The day is dark O make it gold again
Sadly my sweetest Lou I kiss your hand

(trans. D. M. Black)

XLIX from Love and Scorn and Hope (from *Poems to Lou*)

I have held you against my breast like a dove which a little girl crushes unknowingly
I have held you with all your beauty your beauty richer than all the sands of California at the time of the gold rush
I have filled my hunger for sensuality with your smile your looks your trembling
I have even had your pride in my power when I made you bend and you submitted to my dominance
I thought to keep all that it was only a dream
And I am left like Ixion when he had made love to a phantom of cloud in the shape of the goddess called Hera or the unseeable Juno
And who can seize who can grasp cloud who can put his hand on a mirage how he deceives himself thinking he can fill his arms with the blue sky
I thought I could take all your beauty and I have had only your body
The body alas has no eternity
The body has the function of enjoyment but it has no love
And vainly now I try to embrace your spirit
It flees it flees from me in every direction like a knot of snakes disentangling itself
And your sweet arms on the far horizon are serpents the colour of daybreak coiling and coiling in farewell
I am confused I am left bewildered
I am tired of this love which you despise
I feel ashamed of this love which you scorn so much

The body is of no use without the soul
And how can I hope to refind your former body when your soul has gone so far from me
And your body has rejoined your soul
As all living bodies do
O you whom I possessed only dead

And despite everything sometimes I stare into the distance to see if the orderly is coming
I hope as for a joy for your daily letter my heart leaps like a young deer when I see the post-orderly approach
And then I imagine impossible things since your heart isn't with me
And then I imagine that we are going to set out together just us two or perhaps three and no one in the world will ever know anything of our dear journey towards nothing but towards elsewhere and for ever
Over that blue sea more blue than all the blue of the world
Over that sea where no one ever cries Land
For your attending beauty my songs purer than all words would rise even more free than the ocean
Is it too late my heart for that mysterious voyage
Our ship is waiting it is the imagination
And reality will refind us one day
If our souls have refound one another
For this too-beautiful pilgrimage

(trans. D. M. Black)

What's Going On

I'm on guard by the powder magazine
There's a very sweet dog in the sentry box
There are rabbits scampering off into the garrigue
There are some wounded in the guardroom
There's a corporal going around pinching the noses of snorers
There's a corniche road with a view over beautiful valleys
Full of the blossoming trees that give Spring its colour
There are old men talking away in cafés
There's a nurse thinking about me as she sits at the bedside of a wounded soldier
There are great ships out on the wild sea

There's my heart beating time like a bandmaster
There are Zeppelins passing over my mother's home
There's a woman getting on the train in Baccarat
There are gunners sucking acid drops
There are alpine troops camping beneath some storks
There's a 90-millimetre battery firing into the distance
There are so many friends dying in the distance

Always

We will always
Keep going further without ever advancing

And from planet to planet
From nebula to nebula
The Don Juan of a thousand and three comets
Without even stirring from Earth
Looks for new forces
And thinks seriously about ghosts

And so many universes are forgotten
Who then are the great forgetters
Who will know how to make us forget this or that part of the world
Where is the Christopher Columbus to whom we will owe the forgetting of a continent

To lose
But to lose truly
To make way for the lucky find
To lose
Life and find Victory

Exiled Grace

Go on your way my *arc-en-ciel*
Let your bright colours fade from sight
It seems you need this sad exile
Infanta of the bow of light

I cannot see my exiled rainbow
She's slipped across the Pyrenees
But a tricolour flies bravely
Red white blue stream in the breeze

Exiled Grace

Off you go my rainbow girl
Make your many-splendoured dash
Into necessary exile
Infanta of the shot-silk sash

And the rainbow is in exile
Because it can't survive the night
But now I see a flag unfurl
To be my wind-blown Northern Light

(trans. Anne Berkeley)

The Cavalier's Goodbye

God! this soldiering's a delight
We sit around we joke and sing
The north wind and our sighs unite
I keep on polishing this ring

God be with you! The trumpet call!
He trotted off across the rise
And there he died and left his girl
To laugh at fate in her surprise

Palace of the Thunder

Through the opening onto a trench cut into the chalk
Where the wall opposite you looks like nougat
You can see the damp deserted corridor running away to both left and right
And flat on its back a dying shovel whose terrifying face has two regulation eyes so you can hook it under an ammunition wagon
A rat hurries back as I hurry forward
And the trench carries on crowned with chalk and sown with branches
Like a hollow phantom that brings emptiness wherever it goes on its white way
And up above there's a blue roof that makes an excellent lid for a gaze closed off by a few straight lines
But on this side of the opening is a palace that's brand new yet seems old
The ceiling is made from railway sleepers
Between them are pieces of chalk and tufts of pine-needles
And from time to time fragments of chalk fall down like bits of old age

Next to the opening that is closed off by loose cloth like we often use for packing
Lies a hole that serves as a hearth and what burns in this hole is a fire resembling a human soul
It's so swirling so inseparable from what it devours and so evanescent
Iron wires stretch out everywhere supporting the planks like a cross-beam
The wires can also be made into hooks and you can hang thousands of things from them
Just as you hang things from memory
Blue haversacks blue helmets blue ties blue tunics
Bits of sky woven from the purest memories
And sometimes there are vague clouds of chalk that float in the air

On the floorboards shine flares detonators gilded jewels with enamelled heads
Black white red
Tightrope walkers waiting for the moment to set out on their trajectories
And making elegant slender ornaments for this underground home
That is also adorned with six beds in the shape of a horseshoe
Six beds covered with fine blue coats

Above the palace is a high chalk barrow
And sheets of corrugated iron
The frozen river of this ideal domain
But without any water because nothing flows here except the fire that bursts out from melinite
The flowers here are fulminate and this park of ours bursts into blossom from holes left by shells
There's a heap of bells with the soft tones of gleaming cartridge cases
Small elegant pines as in a Japanese landscape
Sometimes the palace is lit by a candle whose flame is as small as a mouse
O tiny palace it's as if we were looking at you through the wrong end of a telescope

Little palace where everything is muffled
Little palace where everything is new and nothing nothing is old
And where everything is precious where everyone is dressed like a king
There's a saddle in one corner straddling a crate
Today's newspaper is lying on the ground
And yet everything appears old in this new home
So old you can understand how men have loved old things
Loved what's well-loved and well-worn
Ever since they lived in caves
Everything there was so precious and new
Everything here is so precious and new
That something older or something which has already been of use
Seems more precious
Than what is new and to hand
In this underground palace that has been hollowed out from such new white chalk
And two new steps
They're not yet two weeks old
Are so old and so worn in this palace which seems antique though it never copies antiquity
That you can see how what's simplest and newest
Is what's closest to so-called antique beauty
While what is weighed down with ornaments
Must age before it can acquire the beauty we call antique
And which is the nobility the strength the ardour the soul the wear and tear
Of what's new and most useful
Of all when it is simple simple
As simple as this little palace of the thunder

To Madeleine

I clasp your memory as it were a real body
And will what my hands might grasp of your beauty
What my hands might one day hold
Will that have any more reality
For who can grasp the magic of Spring
And isn't what can be grasped even less real
Even more fugitive than a memory
Whereas even at a distance a soul can clasp a soul
More deeply and more completely
Than a body can embrace a body
My memory presents you to me
Just as the tableau of Creation
Presented itself to God on the seventh day
Madeleine my dear work
Whom I have brought suddenly to birth
                Your second birth
Nice Les Arcs Toulon Marseille Prunay Wez Thuizy
  Courmelois Beaumont-sur-Vesle
Mourmelon great Cuperly Laval St-Jean-sur-Tourbe Le Mesnil
  Hurlus
Perthes les Hurlus Oran Alger
And I admire my work
We are like stars a long way away from one another
That send one another their light
Remember
How my heart
Was going from door to door like a beggar
And you gave me alms that have enriched me forever
When will I be blackening my gaiters
For the great expedition that will bring me back to you
As you wait for me you wear on your fingers
Poor rings made from aluminium as pale as absence
And as tender as memory
Metal of our love metal like the dawn
O letters dear letters
You wait for mine

And it's my dearest joy
To watch the great plain where the trenches open up like
desire
White trenches pale trenches
And see the post-orderly on his way
Vortexes of flies rise up as he passes
Enemy flies that want to stop him from getting here
I read your letter at once
And set out with you on an infinite pilgrimage
We are alone
And I sing freely and joyfully for you
While your pure voice answers on its own
It's time indeed that this harmony arose
Over the bloody ocean of these poor years
Where day-time is terrible where the sun is the wound
Through which the life of the universe is draining away
It's time Madeleine to weigh anchor

Flashes

The watch is beside the candle that burns quietly behind a
screen made from the tin-plate of a jam tin
In your left hand you hold a stopwatch which you will start
at the correct moment
With your right you are ready to aim the sight alidad at the
far-off flashes
As you do this you start the stopwatch and you stop the
stopwatch when you hear the explosion
You note the time the number of reports the calibre the
bearing the number of seconds elapsed between flash and
detonation
You watch without turning away you watch through the
gun-port
The rockets dance the bombs explode and the flashes flash
While all around can be heard the simple and crude
symphony of the war

So my love in life we bring our heart and our attentive piety to bear
On the unknown and hostile flashes that adorn the horizon and people it and control us
And the poet observes this life and discovers the countless flashes of mysteries that must be located
And known O Flashes O my dearest love

Nothing Much

What a lot of them we've managed to kill
Fuck me
Strange it doesn't mean anything to me
Fuck me
A camembert for the Krauts
Fuck me Fire
A bar of chocolate for the Boches
Fuck me Fire
Each time you say Fire! the word becomes steel and you hear it explode over there
Fuck me
Take cover
Fuck me
Crack!
The buggers are answering back
Strange language isn't it Fuck me

For Madeleine Alone

White moon you shine less than the hips
Of my love
Dawns I admire you are less white
Dawns I admire
Every day O hips so white
A hint of your whiteness
Lies deep in the aluminium
From which we make rings
In this zone where whiteness reigns
O hips so white

Seventh Secret Poem

....

....

I adore you love
I could sing O rapturous Madeleine
        Sing and sing again
            The nightingale that's hidden
There's no ridding the chill the terrible cold
            Under canvas
And I write you the poem I sing as I write
And I write you lying on the ground
            The chill back chill without fire
            Since we're out of wood
I adore you love I'm happy thanks to you
And I take the riches
Of all your body's inches
In one big kiss
Looming up out of winter a feast
            Of purest spring
            The Lily the Rose
            Under my kiss

(trans. Richard Price)

Ninth Secret Poem

I adore your fleece the perfect triangle
        Of the Goddess
I'm the woodcutter in the last virgin forest
        O my El Dorado
I'm the one fish in your voluptuous ocean
        My siren belle
I'm the climber on your snow-laden mountains

O my snowy white Alp
I'm your beautiful lips' immortal bowman
O my darling darling quiver
And I am the hauler of your midnight's hair
O bonny barge plying my kisses' canal
And the lilies of your arms call me to them
O my summer garden
The fruits of your breasts ripen their sweetness for me
O my aromatic orchard
And I lift you up O Madeleine O my beauty up above the world
Like the torch of all light.

(trans. Richard Price)

Eleventh Secret Poem

On everything about you your body your intelligence your reason
I have already written fine poems
And now living as I do in a forest in these days of war
I want to write one about the lovely little hideaway
Deep in virgin forest and so well furnished
The little hideaway you have got ready for me in virgin forest
O palace more splendid than Rosamund's than the Louvre or the Escorial
Where I shall enter to make my finest work of all
I shall be God himself and God willing I shall make a man even several men a woman even several women just as God did himself
O little hidden palace of Madeleine
You are beautiful my love and you are a sublime artist you who are building me the finest palace in the world
Madeleine the architect I worship
I shall throw a bridge between you and me a bridge of flesh hard as iron a bridge suspended miraculously

You the Architect me the Pontiff and creator of Humanity
I worship you Architect and you must worship the builder of the bridge
On it as at Avignon the whole world will dance in a circle
Ourselves O Madeleine our children too and even our grandchildren
Until the end of time

In the Dugout

I hurl myself towards you and I think you hurl yourself towards me too
A force comes from us a solid fire and it welds us together
But then comes an opposing force which stops us from seeing one another
Opposite me the chalk wall's crumbling
There are fractures
Long marks left by tools smooth marks and it's as if they've been cut in tallow
Cracked edges get knocked off by the movements of men from my gun crew
But tonight it's my soul that's hollowed out and empty
It's as if one goes on and on falling there and never finds bottom
And there's nothing to clutch at
What falls there what lives there are ugly beings of some kind they hurt me I don't know where they come from
But I think they come from life from some kind of future life from a raw future that's not yet been cultivated or refined or made human
This great emptiness of my soul lacks a sun it lacks what brings light
That's how it is today this evening not always
Luckily it's only this evening
Other days I cling to you
Other days I find consolation from loneliness and all horrors

Through imagining your beauty
In order to raise it high above the enraptured universe
Then I think I'm imagining it in vain
I don't know your beauty through any of my senses
Nor even through words
Does that make my love of beauty vain too
Do you exist my love
Or are you only an entity I have created without meaning to
So as to people my solitude
Are you a goddess like the goddesses the Greeks created so as to feel less down-hearted
I worship you O my exquisite goddess even if you live only in my imagination

Flare

The black curls on the nape of your neck are my treasure
My thoughts seek you out and your thoughts meet mine
Your breasts are the only shells that I love
Your memory is the searchlight we train on the night

Seeing my horse's broad rump I thought of your hips

The foot soldiers are on their way to the rear they're reading a newspaper

The stretcher-bearer's dog comes back with a pipe in his mouth

A tawny owl fawn wings dull eyes face of a small cat and cat's paws

A green mouse darts through the moss

The rice has burnt in the camp cooking-pot

Which means there are a lot of things you must be careful about

Lengthen the range
Cries the megaphone

Lengthen the range love of your guns

The batteries are balanced in power
Heavy cymbals
Played by cherubim crazy with love
In honour of the God of Armies

A leafless tree on a knoll
The noise of tractors climbing a valley

O old world of the last century with its tall chimneys that are so beautiful and so pure

O great cannons
Manliness of our present century

Exploding charges of 75 millimetre shells
Ring out piously like bells!

Desire

My desire is the region before me
Beyond the Boche lines
My desire is also behind me
Behind the zone of operations

My desire is the Mesnil heights
My desire is what I am firing on
My desire that lies outside the zone of operations
Is something I think of but won't speak of today

Mesnil mound I vainly imagine you
Barbed wire machine guns enemies too sure of themselves
Too well dug in under the ground buried already

The clatter of gunfire dying away in the distance

I lie awake late at night
The light railway coughs

Corrugated iron under the rain
My tin hat under the rain

Listen to the vehement earth
See the flashes before you hear the guns fire

A shell whistling dementedly
Or a tac tac tac that is brief monotonous and full of contempt

I long to grasp you in my hand
Main de Massiges
So thin and bony on the map

I have fired at Goethe's trench
And at Nietzsche's
I'm certainly no respecter of greatness
Night that is violent and violet and dark and at times full of
gold
Night of men only

Night of 24 September
Tomorrow the attack
Violent night O night whose terrible deep cry grows more
intense every minute
Night screaming out like a woman in labour
Night of men only

The Trench

I am the white trench with the white sunken body
And my home is the whole of this devastated earth
Come with me boy enter my sex which is the whole of my body
Come with me penetrate me so I can be happy with bloody voluptuousness
I shall heal your hurts your worries your desires your melancholy
With the clear clean song of the bullets and the orchestra of the artillery
See how white I am whiter than the whitest of bodies
Lie down in my womb as if on a belly you love
I want to give you a love without equal without sleep without words
I've loved so many young men
I love them as Morgan Le Fay loves them
In her castle no one returns from
High up on Mount Gibel
Which is the Etna from which our soldiers rapidly disappear towards Serbia
I've loved them and they are dead and I love only the living
Come on then and enter my sex which is longer than the longest of serpents long as all the bodies of the dead laid end to end
Come and listen to the metallic songs I sing white mouth that I am
Come on the men who love me are there armed with rifles and trench mortars and bombs and grenades and they play there in silence

Wonder of the War

How splendid these flares are that light up the night
They climb up onto their own peak then lean over to have a good look
They're dancing ladies the looks they cast are their eyes arms and hearts

I recognize your smile and your vivacity

They're also the daily apotheosis of all my Berenices whose shocks of hair have turned into comets
These gilded and glittering dancers belong to all times and all races
They give birth abruptly to children who have no time to do anything but die

How fine all these flares are
But it would be even finer if there were more flares
If there were millions of them their meaning complete and coherent like the letters of a book
All the same it's as fine as if life itself were to emerge from the dying

But it would be even finer if there were still more flares
Yet I see them as a beauty who flaunts herself then disappears
I seem to be at a great feast all lit up like the day
The earth is treating herself to a banquet
She is hungry and she opens her long pale mouths
The earth is hungry and she's feasting like Balthasar the cannibal

Who would have guessed we could go so far down the road of anthropophagy
Or that it could take so much fire to roast a human body
That's why the air has a slightly empyreumatic taste that really isn't unpleasant by God

But the feast would be finer still if the sky were feasting along with the earth
All the sky ever swallows is souls
Which is a way of not eating at all
And it's content just to juggle with many-coloured lights

But I and all my company have flowed the length of the long communication trenches and into the sweetness of this war
A few cries of flame keep announcing my presence
I have hollowed out the bed I flow down I branch into a thousand little streams that run everywhere
I am in the trench nearest the enemy and at the same time I am everywhere or rather I am beginning to be everywhere
It is I who am beginning something that belongs to centuries to come
And will take longer to make real than the fable of Icarus the airman

I bequeath to the future the story of Guillaume Apollinaire
Who was in the war and knew how to be everywhere
In the happy towns behind the front line
In all the rest of the universe
In those who die caught in barbed wire
In women in cannon in horses
At the zenith the nadir the four points of the compass
And in the unique ardour of this eve of battle

And doubtless it would be finer still
If I could imagine that all of these things in which I am everywhere
Could enter me too
But in that respect there's nothing doing
For I may be everywhere now but inside me there's still only myself

Exercise

Four bombardiers were on their way
To a small village in the rear
Layers of dust had turned them grey
They'd joined up earlier that year

They quietly spoke of other years
And gazed at the vast plain ahead
A shell coughed near the bombardiers
Not one so much as turned his head

They only talked of yesterday
Tomorrow seemed a waste of breath
They held to their ascetic way
This constant discipline of death

There Is

There's a ship that has taken my love away
There are six sausages in the sky and with night on its way
  they could be maggots about to hatch into stars
There's an enemy submarine that's got it in for my love
There are a thousand little pines shattered by the shell-bursts
  around me
There's a foot soldier who's been blinded by poison gas
There's the way we've really smashed up the Nietzsche,
  Goethe and Cologne trenches
There's my longing for a letter that never comes
There are snapshots of my love inside my wallet
There are prisoners going by with anxious faces
There's a battery whose gunners are bustling about their guns
There's the post-orderly trotting towards us along the path of
  the Lonely Tree

There's said to be a spy prowling about as invisible as the horizon he's cloaked shamelessly round him and which he blends in with
There's a picture of my love as upright as a lily
There's a captain waiting anxiously for wireless bulletins about the Atlantic
There are soldiers at midnight sawing up planks to make coffins
There are women crying out for corn before a bleeding Christ in Mexico
There's the Gulf Stream so warm and benevolent
There's a cemetery full of crosses five kilometres away
There are crosses all over the place
There are Barbary figs on the cacti in Algeria
There are my love's long supple hands
There's an inkwell I made from a 15-centimetre rocket they didn't send off
There's my saddle outside in the rain
There are rivers that don't flow back uphill
There's love carrying me away with its sweetness
There was a Boche prisoner carrying his machine-gun on his back
There are men in the world who have never seen war
There are Hindus gazing astonished at our Western campaigns
They think sadly about people they fear they may never see again
For the art of invisibility has been taken a long way in this war

Listen to the Rain Listen to the Rain (from Cotton in Your Ears)

then
lis
ten
to
the
rain
lis
ten
to
the
swe
et
and
ten
der
rain

sol
di
ers
who
are
lo
st
and
bl
ind
a
mid
the
bar
bed
wi
re
and
un
der
the
li
quid
moon

of
Flan
ders
in
a
g
o
n
y
un
der
the
fi
ne
rain
un
der
the
swe
et
and
ten
der
rain

be
one
with
the
ho
ri
zon
beau
ti
ful
and
in
vi
si
ble
be
ings
un
der
the
fi
ne
rain

un
der
the
swe
et
rain
un
der
the
swe
et
and
ten
der
rain

(fragment)

Harden yourself old heart hear the piercing cries
Let out by the wounded in agony in the distance
Men lice of the earth O tenacious vermin

from Honour's Song

. . .
But here as elsewhere I know that beauty
Is mostly just a matter of simplicity
Here in the trenches I've seen so many dead
Still standing on their feet leaning their heads
Quite straightforwardly against the parapet
Once I saw four men killed by the same shell
They stood there a long time dead unbowed
Just slightly leaning like four Pisan towers

Ten days in mud and mud-slides rain and cold
We've waited hidden in a narrow trench
With flesh all round us painful rotting flesh
As we tensely guard the Tahure road

An octopus has three hearts to suffer with
But all yours beat in me I feel each wound
My wounded soldiers comrades close to death

The night is so beautiful a bullet coos
And a river of shells flows over our heads
Sometimes the whole night is lit up by a flare
A flower that blossoms instantly and fades
The earth's lamenting now and like the tide
A wave of song climbs up to my chalk lair
Home of insomnia uncertain abode
Of night alarms fierce itching and of Death
. . .

Platoon Commander

My mouth will have all the fires of Gehenna
You will find my mouth a hell of sweetness and seduction
My mouth's angels will reign in your heart
My mouth's soldiers will take you by storm
My mouth's priests will burn incense before your beauty
Your soul will tremble like the earth in an earthquake
Your eyes will be filled with all the love that has gathered in people's eyes since humanity came into being
My mouth will be an army against you an army of rebels
Protean as a sorcerer who knows how to vary his metamorphoses
The orchestra and the choirs of my mouth will tell you my love
My mouth murmurs to you now from far away
As I keep my eyes on my watch and wait for the moment we go over the top

Shadow

Here you are near me again
Memories of my companions who have died in the war
Olive of time
Memories that make only one memory
As a hundred furs make only one coat
As these thousands of wounds make only one newspaper article
Dark and intangible as you are
You have taken on
The changing form of my shadow
A Red Indian lying in wait throughout eternity
Shadow
You creep about near me

But you no longer hear me
You will no longer know the divine poems I sing
Though as for me I can hear you I can still see you
Destinies
Multiple shadow
May the sun watch over you
You who love me enough never to leave me
You who dance in the sun yet raise no dust
Shadow
Ink of the sun
Handwriting of my light
Ammunition wagon of regrets
A god humbling himself

The Pretty Redhead

Here I am before you all a man of good sense
Knowing life and as much as the living can know of death
Having been through the pains and joys of love
And having managed now and again to make people respect my ideas
Knowing several languages
Having travelled widely
Having seen war with the Artillery and the Infantry
And been wounded in the head and trepanned under chloroform
Having lost my best friends in the terrible struggle
I know both old and new as much as one man can ever hope to
And without worrying for the moment about this war
Between ourselves my friends and for ourselves
I shall judge this long quarrel between tradition and invention
Between Order and Adventure

You whose mouth is made in the image of God's
Mouth that is order itself

Be indulgent when you compare us
To those who were the perfection of order
Us who seek everywhere for adventure

We are not your enemies
We want to give you vast and strange worlds
Where flowering mystery yields to whoever wants to pick it
Where there are new fires colours never seen before
A thousand weightless phantoms
That must be made real
We want to explore kindness that vast country where all is silent
And then there is time that can be banished or recalled
Pity us who are always fighting on the frontiers
Of infinity and the future
Pity our mistakes pity our sins

Summer's on the way season of violence
And like the Spring my youth is dead
Now O sun it is the time of ardent reason
And I intend
To follow for ever the sweet and noble form
She's taken on so I'll love her and no one else
Here she comes drawing me after her as a magnet draws iron
And she is lovely
And has red hair

Her hair is gold it's like
A lightning flash that doesn't stop
Or the flames that go on glowing
In a fading rose

But laugh laugh at me
Men everywhere especially people here
For there are so many things I'm afraid to tell you
So many things you'd never let me tell you
Have pity on me

Part Four

Views of Apollinaire

BLAISE CENDRARS

from Homage to Guillaume Apollinaire

. . .
Times pass
Years flow by like clouds
The soldiers have gone back
To their homes
In their country
And now a new generation is rising
The dream of TIRESIAS'S BREASTS is coming true
Little French people half English half Black half Russian a
little Belgian Italian Annamite Czech
One with a Canadian accent one with Hindu eyes
Teeth face bones joints figure gait smile
They've all got something foreign about them and all belong
here
And amid them, Apollinaire, sprawled out like that statue of
the Nile, father of waters, small children welling up
From between his feet, under his arm-pits, out of his beard
They look like their father yet go their own way
And they all speak the language of Apollinaire.

(Paris, November 1918)

MADELEINE PAGÈS

from *Tender as Memory*

It was on 1 January 1915, in the train taking me back from Nice to Marseille, that I met Guillaume Apollinaire. I had just spent Christmas in Nice, with the family of my elder brother, a second lieutenant in the artillery. And I was going back to Oran by the boat which would be leaving Marseille that evening, the *Sidi-Brahim*, I think.

I was happy. I had enjoyed my holiday. My suitcase was full of presents that I was taking back to my mother, and to the sisters and little brothers who would be waiting for me. I was very proud of the pretty hat I was wearing. And it was a glorious morning.

Buying my ticket for the eight o'clock train, choosing a second-class compartment right in the middle of the carriage – everything had gone smoothly and easily. And so I climbed confidently aboard, lifted my suitcase up onto the rack, and put my book, my paper and my sandwiches on the seat beside me.

There was no one in the station except for the few employees on duty. I was comfortably settled in my corner, looking forward to having the compartment to myself all the way to Marseille, when a soldier came in, murmured an apology as he stepped in front of me, and leaned out of the window to talk to a lady who was seeing him off. Was he a soldier or an officer? I've never been able to recognize ranks. He was tall – yes, quite tall – but his legs were a little short and he was barrel-chested. His képi was too small and he wore it pushed back on his head.

So much for my solitude. I would have moved to the next compartment, only I didn't want to draw attention to myself. But the soldier was saying something in a soft voice: 'Poetry?

If you want to read poetry, then read Baudelaire's *Fleurs du Mal*.'

Had he really said 'Baudelaire's *Fleurs du Mal*'? I would stay where I was.

The lady came into the compartment for a moment, to say goodbye. She was tall and slim, and seemed a little tired; so as not to get in the way, I slipped quickly out into the corridor.

The lady got off. I went back to my place. Then I heard the voice of the soldier again. He was leaning out of the window, saying, 'Don't hang about on the platform getting cold. Go back to the room – it's paid for till twelve.'

The train pulled out. Now the morning was even finer. The carriage was well heated. I smiled to myself as I thought of all the little things in my suitcase and how delighted my sisters would be when they saw them. I wanted someone to share my thoughts with.

There was the little pink beach with its pines that I had gone to last year with my brother, when he was getting married. *There* was the sea. How very beautiful it was. I must have said something out loud – the soldier had left his corner and was now standing beside me. We looked at the sea together, suddenly united by our shared joy in its beauty and blueness.

We spoke of Nice, which we had just left and which he knew better than I did . . . I liked his slightly husky voice. I liked his profile and the lazy movements of his ringless hands. He gave me a quick look, which made me feel good . . .

By now I was completely at ease. I smiled as we talked and, whenever I glanced up, I found he was looking at me. His eyes were chestnut, like his hair. He had a splendid face; now that he'd taken off his képi, he really looked handsome. Suddenly it was ten o'clock. Blushing considerably, I offered my travelling companion a sandwich, which he accepted graciously. We both ate; the train was going faster now, the rhythm made us feel happy and carefree, and somehow, I can't quite remember how, we began to talk about poets. I think he asked me if I liked poetry as he was swallowing a slice of ham, and I answered that I loved poetry as much as life itself, that to me they were one and the same thing. He was so pleased that I thought he was going to kiss me; I felt there was something he wanted to tell me, but he changed his mind and began talking about particular poets. He wanted to know who I knew, who I liked; soon we were laughing, mentioning names and quoting lines that we knew by heart:

Voici des fruits, des fleurs, des feuilles et des branches,[1]

Sois sage, ô ma douleur, et tiens-toi plus tranquille[2]

Some we recited together, suddenly standing by the door and looking out at the coast. It too was young, and the sea was sparkling.

Sur le printemps de ma jeunesse folle
Je ressemblais a l'arondelle qui vole . . .[3]

'Do you know Villon, Mademoiselle? I love him.'

Entranced, I immediately came out with the lines:
Femme, je suis povrette et ancienne.
Qui rien ne sçay; oncques lettre ne leuz . . .[4]

[1] The first line of a famous poem by Verlaine, 'Green': 'Here are fruits and flowers, leaves and branches'.

[2] The first line of a poem by Baudelaire: 'Be calm, my sorrow, and don't take things so hard'.

[3] 'In the Spring of my mad youth I was like a flying swallow'. I have been unable to trace this, which sounds like a pastiche of François Villon.

[4] from François Villon: 'I am a woman, poor and old, and I know nothing. I don't know letters'.

But the poetry had somehow made us more serious, and I had withdrawn dreamily into my corner, closing my eyes.

The lines he had spoken were resonating inside me; I had never before understood quite how wonderful they were. It was as if he had been holding them in his hand, enjoying their feel as much as their sound. And yet he spoke them, or rather murmured them, with a simplicity I was unable to match. Astonished, overcome, I had let him finish lines I had begun myself.

The train stopped at Fréjus and another passenger came in to our compartment. How sad! But I didn't feel like talking, and I folded my hands demurely across my closed book.

The new passenger sat down opposite us; the soldier hadn't moved at all, as if to give the impression that he was travelling with me. I was a little uncomfortable at being found on such close terms with a stranger.

The soldier was unhappy – I could tell from the way he was fidgeting about beside me. I felt sorry that I was upsetting him and, after a moment, I turned towards him and smiled. His answering smile was so shy, so charming, that I felt quite disturbed by it. Never before, I felt, had I been enveloped by such tender admiration. But the new passenger began talking to the soldier . . .

The passenger left the train . . . The soldier took my closed book and toyed with it for a moment. Gradually he began to talk about poetry again, about how much it can express and how it can give life to things. Then he began a game of finding an image for each of the towns we had been through.

Nice, he said, was a rearing horse, a thoroughbred horse rearing up in the middle of some celebration, surrounded by the hubbub of a carnival and flowers being thrown in the air.

I saw Villefranche as a great shell, wide open to the sea and the sky.

Very softly, as though picking up a much earlier thread of our conversation, he murmured: 'I am a poet too, Mademoiselle. I write under the pseudonym of Guillaume Apollinaire. Have you heard of me?'

A poet! He was a poet! 'Wait till I tell everyone at home!' I said to myself. I was breathless with joy, but I had to answer, in a thin awkward voice, that I had not yet heard of him.

He was surprised. 'In Algeria you seem to be so well informed about poetry that I thought . . .'

'Perhaps I should admit that most of what I know about contemporary poets comes from a little selection that costs fifteen sous and is called: *The Hundred Best French Poems*. And there isn't yet a poem of yours in my little book.'

He assured me that it seemed to be a very good selection anyway, judging from what I'd learned by heart. 'But I'd like to show you my own poems. I'll send you a volume, *Alcohols*, which was published in 1913. And you must let me know what you think of it.' I thanked him with a nod and a smile.

His name now seemed so familiar that I began to feel quite unsure of myself. Guillaume Apollinaire! How could I have told him that I didn't know his name? I began to feel certain that his name had jumped out at me one morning from a newspaper and that I'd liked it. The bold play on the name of Apollo had amused me . . .

We were coming into Marseille. It was time to put on my hat – the poet was holding it out to me. Standing in front of the mirror, I fluffed up my hair and looked with astonishment at the new face I saw there: a little pale, the eyes too big. But then, behind my own face, I saw the poet's; his eyes were smiling, following my movements, and for the first time since Nice I was able to take a long look at him . . .

As I was lowering my veil, our eyes met in the mirror and I smiled at him, enchanted by the tenderness and attentiveness with which he was looking at me, flustered by a rush of feeling all trace of which had to be banished from my eyes before I left the mirror and turned round . . .

CHRISTOPHER REID

Apollinaire

(from *Katerina Brac*)

As gratuitous as flowers
in the iconography of children,
bombs exploded
on the blank sheet of his mind.

When you gave me his poems,
the strangely fragrant French edition,
I was terrified
by such *boutades* of innocence.

An animating principle
that was not the same as morality
declared itself as I read those pages
full of love and war.

As if the god of the old superstitions
had taken a holiday
under an assumed name,
wearing a jaunty bow-tie.

Picasso drew him
in the form of a coffeepot,
but that was just one of his many
ingenious metamorphoses.

His exotic name suggests
that he was related to Apollo –
or Apollo himself, condemned
to drudge for a while in France.

Surely that would account
for the supererogatory Golden Age
of artistic abundance
when the whole of Paris turned Cubist.

Under his divine inspiration
poems became pictures
of hearts, stars, guns –
everything that they should not be.

I still have your book:
it stays mainly on its shelf,
but I pick it up from time to time
when I want to give myself a fright.

ROBERT CHANDLER

After Guillaume Apollinaire(y)

Because he was born in Tipperary
At a time when donkeys were rare, he
Travelled the world on a dromedary.
I don't have a dromedary,
But I've travelled his itinerary.

Notes

Tortoise: Orpheus was born in Thrace and played a lyre, made from the shell of a tortoise, that he had been given by Hermes. His singing and playing enchanted even wild animals. *The Bestiary*, from which this group of poems is selected, was illustrated by Raoul Dufy. The poems and Dufy's woodcuts match perfectly; many of the poems are extremely visual, and the incisiveness of Dufy's line complements that of Apollinaire's verse. Some of the poems were set to music in 1919 by Poulenc. 'Louse' was published only posthumously.

Ibis: *Ibis* is the Latin for 'you shall go'.

Le Pont Mirabeau: First published in February 1912, this was probably written as Apollinaire's affair with Marie Laurencin was coming to an end. It is the most famous poem from his second book, *Alcohols* (1913). The second section of the present volume includes: first, a selection from *Alcohols*; second, a few poems published only posthumously; and third, the pre-war poems from *Calligrams* (1917).

Meadow Saffron: The French title is *Les Colchiques* – after Colchis, the birthplace of Medea. Apollinaire imagines he is being poisoned, in a Rhineland meadow, by frustrated love for Annie Playden.

Dusk: Picasso's paintings of this date are also full of harlequins. In 1905, Apollinaire wrote of Picasso: 'Beneath the tawdry finery of his slender clowns, one feels the presence of real young men of the people, versatile, shrewd, clever, poor, and deceitful.' Garnet Rees writes of this poem: 'The marked absence of colour . . . adds to its unreality and seems to be a description of Marie Laurencin's own discreet pastels' (*Alcools*, ed. Garnet Rees, London, Athlone, 1975, p. 139). 'Hermes-Pierrot of the Book' ('l'arlequin trismégiste' in the original) is a reference to Hermes Trismegistus, a legendary ancient Egyptian believed to have composed several important magical texts.

Annie: Annie Playden had moved to America, at least partly to escape Apollinaire's attentions. The town of Mobile is in fact in Alabama, not

Texas. Some Mennonite communities did indeed fasten their clothes with hooks rather than buttons.

The House of the Dead: Apollinaire visited Munich in 1902. At this time corpses waiting to be buried were displayed behind glass. This poem was first published as a short story, in prose.

Cortège: Cornelius Agrippa, the sixteenth-century philosopher and occultist, was moved by his admiration of St Ursula to write a treatise on the superiority of women. According to legend, Ursula and eleven thousand virgin companions were massacred in Cologne by the Huns.

Poem Read at the Wedding of André Salmon: Apollinaire claimed to have written this on the open upper deck of a bus, on his way to the wedding. It was 13 July 1903, and Paris was festooned with flags for the Quatorze Juillet. Apollinaire jotted the poem down while a friend chattered beside him. He, however, liked to make out that his poetry was more spontaneous than was actually the case. Apollinaire and Salmon first met in 1902, at a *soirée* held in the Café du Départ. A *moujik* is a Russian peasant: Salmon had lived for some time in Russia. Salmon has explained that the cellar was 'accursed' because it was a meeting place for 'young men devoting themselves to poetry, which is a dangerous activity'. The word also alludes to the nineteenth-century *poètes maudits*: Corbière, Mallarmé, Rimbaud, Verlaine and others.

The Gypsy Woman: Another poem about Apollinaire's love for Annie Playden.

The Brazier: Amphion built the walls of Thebes through the power of music; the sounds of his lyre drew the stones into place.

The Lorelei: Adapted from a ballad by the German Romantic, Clemens Brentano, this incorporates more personal themes. Annie Playden was often told by her family that her eyes were 'perverse' and had an evil power of fascination.

1909: Mme Récamier (1777–1849) was a famous beauty and society hostess during the reign of Napoleon and under the Restoration. She was painted by David.

Inside: The French title is 'A La Santé' – 'In La Santé Prison'. Apollinaire spent five days there, suspected of stealing the *Mona Lisa* from the Louvre. This undermined his self-confidence and sense of identity. As a foreign citizen, he could have been exiled for life. The poem contains allusions to poems written in prison by Verlaine.

Inscription for the Tomb of the Painter Henri Rousseau the Customs Inspector: Monsieur Queval was Rousseau's landlord. A well-known painting by Rousseau, *La muse inspirant le poète*, portrays Apollinaire standing beside Marie Laurencin.

The Windows: Written in 1913 for a catalogue of paintings by Robert Delaunay, the Orphic Cubist, who in 1912 had painted a series entitled 'Windows'. The poem can be seen as a literary equivalent of Delaunay's prismatic colours, each brief improvisation presenting a contrasting facet of experience. The pihi is an imaginary Chinese one-winged bird that flies in pairs. In the West Indies the children of marriages between Negroes and mulattoes are called Chabins or Chabines.

Monday on Christine Street: Admired by such later innovators as the Surrealists. With its multiple and fragmented perspectives, this too can be thought of as a 'Cubist' poem.

A Phantom of Cloud: The title can best be explained by the first ten lines of 'Love and Scorn and Hope' (p. 56). Longwy is a town in eastern France. The description of the child acrobat is inspired by early Picasso, above all by the paintings *Circus Family* and *Young Acrobat on a Ball*.

The Little Car: In the original the lines 'I shall never . . . a burst tyre' are laid out to form the shape of a car. The third section of the present volume includes war poems published only posthumously, as well as war poems from *Calligrammes*. I have tried to arrange the poems in chronological order, though this is not always easy to establish.

At Nîmes: The Greek *Nike* means *Victory*. Apollinaire enlisted in Nice on 4 December 1914, then joined a field artillery regiment in Nîmes. He underwent first basic training, then officer training. On 4 April 1915 he gave up the latter and asked to be transferred to a fighting unit. *Le Charroi de Nîmes* ('The Transport of Nîmes') is the title of a twelfth-century epic or *chanson de geste*, which Apollinaire imagines is being re-enacted. He probably knew that *Le Charroi de Nîmes* belongs to the same cycle of these epics as *Le Chanson de Guillaume.*

Because You Spoke to Me of Vice: One of many poems sent by Apollinaire, first from Nîmes and then from the front, to Louise de Coligny ('Lou'). Some of these poems were included, often with revisions, in *Calligrammes.* The other seventy-six were published posthumously as *Poèmes à Lou.*

What's Going On: Norma Rinsler writes:

> The only way to avoid fear was not to think of the future at all. . . . Concentration on the present moment magnifies all the details of a man's surroundings. He will generally try to make them fill the range of his vision, excluding that other world which would make plain their horror or strangeness. The result is a fragmentation of consciousness: all details are equally significant, and there is no attempt to place them in a meaningful pattern: it is precisely their meaning which the soldier is trying to ignore. Apollinaire succeeds in recreating this state of mind by simple juxtaposition; a number of observed, remembered and imagined details are placed side by side, introduced flatly by 'Il y a . . .', so that all are separate and equal.
>
> ('The War Poems of Apollinaire', *French Studies*, April 1971: 178)

Exiled Grace: One of seven poems intended to accompany drawings by Marie Laurencin, though she seems to have let the project drop. After breaking with Apollinaire, Marie married a German painter, moving to Spain with him for the duration of the war. Marie is seen here as exotic and ethereal. I have left the word *arc-en-ciel* untranslated; it means rainbow.

The Cavalier's Goodbye: The ironic first line ('Ah Dieu! que la guerre est jolie') has been quoted out of context in support of the absurd view that Apollinaire saw the war simply as a spectacle to be enjoyed. The ring being polished would have been a fragment of aluminium from a shell. Soldiers often occupied themselves in their dugouts with making rings for their sweethearts. Cf. 'To Madeleine', p. 63.

Flashes: Included in a letter to Madeleine of September 1915, prefaced by the words: 'You asked me what it's like being an observer. Here's a little poem about it' (Apollinaire, *Tendre comme le souvenir*, Paris: Gallimard, 1952, p. 136).

The Secret Poems: From a series of poems sent to Madeleine from the front and published only posthumously. Rosamund Clifford, the mistress of Henry II of England, had a palace at Woodstock. The Escorial was built for Philip II of Spain.

In the Dugout: An earlier version ended with three more lines:

But you exist Madeleine your beauty is real
I adore you
In spite of the sadness of the chalk and the brutality of the unending cannon fire.

The Trench: In late 1915, shortly before this poem was sent to Madeleine, French toops were sent to Serbia. They sailed via Marseille and the Straits of Messina, passing Mount Etna.

Wonder of the War: Bérénice was an Egyptian princess. A lock of her hair is said to have formed the constellation of Coma Berenices. As the heroine of a tragedy by Racine, she stands for the ideal of pure love. A fine translation of this poem by Robert Garioch is included in his *Collected Poems*. Norma Rinsler has written with particular reference to the penultimate stanza: '[Apollinaire's] imaginative sympathy ... made him incapable of sustained insensibility, which is a defence by exclusion. His more characteristic solution was one of inclusion: he links himself through love with civilians and soldiers, animals and machines, life and death' (op. cit., p. 181).

Listen to the Rain Listen to the Rain: A short extract from 'Cotton in Your Ears'. The rest of the poem is dense with calligraphic complexity and untranslatable word-play.

Platoon Commander: Cf. these lines from a letter to Madeleine: 'The horrible, tragic, sombre horror of hand-to-hand fighting in the trenches and shell-holes increases the voluptuous love I feel for you.' (My translation of a passage quoted in *Calligrammes*, trans. Anne Hyde Greet, University of California Press, 1991, p. 495.)

Homage to Guillaume Apollinaire: Blaise Cendrars (1887–1961) was a friend of Apollinaire's. *Tiresias's Breasts* is the title of a play that Apollinaire wrote in 1917.

Tender as Memory: From the preface to *Tendre comme le souvenir*, a volume containing Apollinaire's letters and poems to Madeleine Pagès. Madeleine writes with unusual delicacy and fluency; these pages proved as hard to translate as Apollinaire's own poems.

Apollinaire: From *Katerina Brac* (London: Faber & Faber, 1985). The word *boutade* has several meanings, all relevant: (1) whim, caprice; (2) sudden outburst; (3) sally, flash of wit.

Acknowledgements

The editor and publishers wish to thank the following for permission to use copyright material:

The Saltire Society for Robert Garioch, 'Autumn' from *Complete Poetical Works* by Robert Garioch.

Earlier versions of several of Robert Chandler's own translations were first published in *Modern Poetry in Translation* and *The Times Literary Supplement*. The translations by Harry Guest were first published in *Versions* (Odyssey Poets, Nether Stowey, 1999), those by William Meredith in *Alcools* (Doubleday, New York, 1964), those by Richard Price in *Eftirs/Afters* (Au Quai, Glasgow, 1996); the poem and the adaptation by Christopher Reid were first published in *All Sorts* (Ondt and Gracehoper, 161 York Way, London N7).

Every effort has been made to trace the copyright holders but if any have been inadvertently overlooked the publishers will be pleased to make the necessary arrangements at the first opportunity.